CARNATIONS
AND PINKS

RICHARD BIRD

COLLINS

Products mentioned in this book

Benlate* + 'Activex'	contains	benomyl
'Fumite' General Purpose Insecticide Smoke	contains	pirimiphos-methyl
'Keriroot'	contains	NAA + captan
'Picket'	contains	permethrin
'Rapid'	contains	pirimicarb
'Sybol'	contains	pirimiphos-methyl
'Weedol'	contains	diquat/paraquat

Products marked thus *'Sybol'* are trade marks of Imperial Chemical Industries plc
Benlate* is a registered trade mark of Du Pont's
Read the label before you buy: use pesticides safely.

Editors Maggie Daykin, Susanne Mitchell
Designer Chris Walker
Picture research Moira McIlroy

First published 1988 by
William Collins Sons & Co Ltd
London · Glasgow · Sydney
Auckland · Toronto · Johannesburg

© Marshall Cavendish Limited 1988

British Library Cataloguing in Publication Data

Bird, Richard
    Carnations and pinks. —— (Collins Aura
    garden handbooks).
    1. Carnations 2. Pinks
    I. Title
    635.9'33152   SB413.C3

    ISBN 0–00–412380–8

Photset by Bookworm Typesetting
Printed and bound in Hong Kong by Dai Nippon Printing
Company

Front cover: Dianthus 'Christopher' by Michael Warren
Back cover: Dianthus barbatus by The Harry Smith Horticultural
Photographic Collection

CONTENTS

INTRODUCTION

Few garden plants have the universal appeal of pinks and carnations. This runs from the formality of a wedding buttonhole to the informality of a crowded cottage garden. They appeal to all the senses — beauty to the eye, fragrance to the nose and even taste to the palate, since in medieval times they were used to flavour wines and food.

An old Malmaison carnation. These are grown in the same way as perpetual-flowering carnations and modern varieties are available. They are highly scented.

'Laced Romeo' is one of the Tudor laced pinks, an old and hardy group. This variety flowers freely and has large blooms.

These plants have been appreciated for such a long time that the beginnings of their history are lost in the mists of time. Their generic name, *Dianthus*, derived from the ancient Greeks' description of them, means 'divine flower', a description with which few would disagree.

They have been grown in this country since at least Norman times when *Dianthus caryophyllus* was introduced. This species and *D. plumarius* are two basic ingredients of the very mixed parentage of our modern carnations and pinks. The story is one of continual development. By Tudor times they had been separated into the two groups that we now call border carnations and old-fashioned pinks. By the seventeenth century they were at the height of their popularity, but during the late eighteenth century there was a renewed surge of interest with the development of new varieties of laced pinks.

The nineteenth century saw the introduction of Remontant carnations, forebears of the perpetual-flowering carnation. Their great popularity has not waned during the twentieth century either. Montagu Allwood introduced his famous Allwoodii pinks which fathered the new generation of modern pinks, and other growers have constantly added even more, noteworthy new varieties to all groups of carnation.

The general appearance of the different types of carnation does not vary much, so it can be difficult for the uninitiated to tell them apart. The true difference lies less in variations in appearance, than in the way they are grown and their frequency of flowering.

Types of carnation
(from left to right):
Modern pink
Perpetual-flowering
carnation
Annual carnation
Border carnation

Border carnations These are hardy carnations that can be grown in an open border. Although they need renewing from time to time, they can be considered perennial. They have only one flowering period during the year – July in the South of the country and slightly later in the North.

There are three main groups of border carnations: selfs, which are flowers of one colour; picotees, which have a single overall colour (either white or yellow) with each petal delicately edged with a contrasting colour; and fancies which consist of flakes and bizarres. This last group was very popular in Elizabethan times; they are multicoloured carnations spotted or streaked in one or more colours over the main colour of the petals.

Perpetual-flowering carnations
These are tender and have to be grown under glass, but have the advantage of flowering all the year round. A little bit of heat is required to coax them to bloom through the winter, but if blooms are not required they will survive in a cool greenhouse without flowering. These are the carnations commonly seen in florists' windows and used in buttonholes and bouquets. Because of their association with weddings they are often thought of as white flowers, but there is a wide range of colours, including aptly-named fancies which are either striped or speckled.

ABOVE Perpetual-flowering carnations can be made to flower all the year round if a little heat is provided in the winter.

LEFT Annual carnations are raised from seed each year and discarded after flowering. They make a marvellous show in summer when mass planted in beds.

LEFT The modern pink 'Little Jock' is a miniature variety, which makes it ideal for the rock garden.

ABOVE 'Paddington' is a dwarf double laced pink with a most attractive deep maroon centre.

American spray carnations These are not yet widely grown in this country but are gaining in popularity, particularly as cut flowers as they are long lasting. As their name implies, they carry four to six blooms on each stem, rather than the more usual one per stem. A wide range of colours is becoming available, and this includes both single and multicoloured blooms.

Annual carnations All carnations and pinks are really perennial, but some are better treated as annuals. They are raised from seed each year, then discarded after flowering, just like other bedding plants. They have the same advantage as the perpetuals in that they flower for a long period, from July to the first frosts, yet like the border carnations they can be grown outside. But their useful life is short and they do not last quite so long as cut flowers in water as the other types. The main strain is known either as 'Chabaud' carnations, after the Frenchman who first raised them, or 'Marguerite' carnations as he named them. 'Grenadin' is another strong strain which is gaining in popularity.

9

Sweet Williams are popular as bedding plants, flowering in early summer. Today there are dwarf strains available. They are raised from seeds sown in early summer.

Old-fashioned pinks These are among the best-loved of garden plants, evocative of summery cottage gardens. They are hardy perennial plants smaller in all their parts than carnations. They are usually grown in rock gardens or at the front of herbaceous borders, often spilling over paths or patios. The old-fashioned varieties flower once only, in the early summer. A variety of forms and shades is available: singles, doubles, fringed and plain petals, single or bicoloured. Most have an 'eye', sometimes of a strong contrasting colour, while the 'laced' varieties have coloured edges. Their strong scent is a welcome bonus.

Modern pinks Modern pinks are the result of hybridizing during the present century. They resemble the old-fashioned pinks in many respects but tend to be larger in flower and less compact in growth. The flowers are often brighter coloured and some of them lack scent, but they have the great advantage that their flowering period extends throughout the summer and into autumn. They make a grand display in the garden and are excellent as cut flowers.

The first of the modern hybrids were the Allwoodii pinks, raised at Allwood's nursery, which still produces new varieties. These highly scented hybrids were raised by crossing perpetual-flowering carnations with old-fashioned pinks. They have themselves been used as the basis of other modern pinks, including Show Pinks and London Pinks.

Species These valuable, compact, dwarf plants are usually grown in a rock garden, in troughs, or even dry stone walls. They are mainly selected forms derived from seed of wild species which have not been too much 'improved' by hybridizing. Two species which are quite different from the rest are the Sweet Williams (*Dianthus barbatus*) and Japanese pinks (*D. chinensis*) which are popularly used as bedding plants or even in herbaceous borders.

OUTDOOR CULTIVATION

Growing carnations and pinks is neither difficult nor time-consuming. Outdoor varieties are particularly easy and demand little special attention. Indoor varieties are slightly more demanding as they need housing in an airy greenhouse and can be more prone to pests and diseases if simple hygiene measures are not attended to.

Modern pinks and border carnations are ideal for growing at the front of herbaceous or mixed borders but require a position in full sun.

Border carnations and pinks need a sunny position with as much air and light as possible. Choose a site which gets the maximum available sun during the day. They are reasonably tolerant plants, so if your garden is sunless you can still get good results provided they are not overshadowed by trees, hedges or walls. For the best results carnations should be grown in a border by themselves. If planted in a mixed border it is very easy for them to become overshadowed and swamped by their lusher neighbours. This not only prevents light from reaching their leaves, but also causes the base of the plants to rot as air does not circulate freely. Pinks can be grown at the front of a border where any companion plants will also be low growers. A well constructed rock garden is an ideal site in which to grow the species and the smaller, delicate pinks.

Soil Carnations and pinks flourish best in lighter soils as they like to be as well drained as possible. Wetness round the roots and base of the plants is fatal. There seems to be a preference for a neutral soil (pH in the region of 6.5 to 7) but they will tolerate most soils except those which are very acid. The ground should be well dug, preferably double dug, and any perennial weeds removed by hand or killed with 'Weedol' before digging even begins. If you garden on heavy soil, mix in drainage material such as broken rubble, horticultural grit or sharp sand when digging. Avoid creating a sump, by ensuring that water can drain away from the bottom of the bed, otherwise the surrounding area will drain into your prepared ground. If the ground is really heavy and tends to become waterlogged, you will need to install a proper land-drainage system.

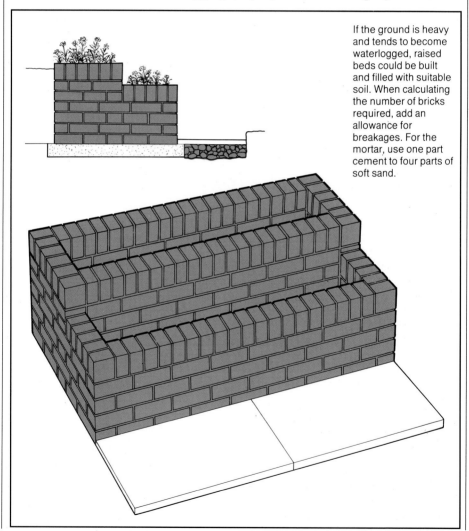

If the ground is heavy and tends to become waterlogged, raised beds could be built and filled with suitable soil. When calculating the number of bricks required, add an allowance for breakages. For the mortar, use one part cement to four parts of soft sand.

LEFT A delightful pink and blue colour scheme in a mixed border, with pinks in the foreground.

BELOW Pinks and border carnations combine beautifully with silver and grey foliage plants and both need the same conditions of full sun and very well-drained soil.

A cheaper and very effective method is to build raised beds filled with soil of your own choice. You can easily construct 30cm (1ft) high walls from stone, brick or timber and fill the bed with the best loam you can obtain. If you have to use soil from your own garden, improve it as much as you can by adding drainage material and organic matter, such as peat or well rotted garden compost.

Raised beds have a particular advantage for growing pinks and *Dianthus* species as the extra height not only improves the drainage but raises the plants nearer to the eye and the nose so that they are better appreciated. Carnations and pinks dislike very acid soils, but this presents few problems as lime can be added when the bed is prepared. Alternatively, less acid soil can be introduced into the bed.

LEFT Small-growing pinks of all kinds, together with thymes and other mat-forming plants, are ideal subjects for planting in paving.

BELOW The Allwoodii pink 'Mandy', in two shades of pink, is a very free-flowering variety and highly recommended.

Planting Give as much attention to planting carnations as to soil preparation. The first question is when to plant. The best time is probably in autumn when the soil is still warm enough for the plants to become established before winter sets in. If autumn is excessively wet or cold, it might be better to wait until spring, overwintering the plants under glass. If you are not raising the plants yourself, order them from a nursery in plenty of time, so that you have them when you are ready to plant and to ensure that you have the varieties you require.

It is best to prepare the bed well in advance, preferably in spring, so that the weather has time to break down the soil and you have had a chance to remove any persistent weeds that escaped your attention while digging. If the ground is very dry, give it a good soaking the day before you plant out. Likewise the plants in their pots should be thoroughly watered then allowed to drain.

Planting distances are a matter of personal choice – 30cm (1ft) should be the minimum, but if you want more room to move between the plants or intend keeping them for several years, allow 45–60cm (1½–2ft) between them. If they are planted in mixed herbaceous borders, ensure that they are far enough from other plants so they are not smothered or overshadowed when the border is in full leaf.

Avoid planting them too deep. Set them in the ground with the top of the root ball level with the surface of the bed. Firm the plants in the ground and make sure that no cavity is left under or round the side of their roots. Water them in well.

Plant pinks and the species at the same time and in the same way as carnations. The distance between plants will be less: 20–30cm (10–12in) for pinks and 15–30cm (6–12in) for species. When planting them in raised beds or rock gardens it is a good idea to surround the plants with a mulch of gravel or limestone chippings. This helps to keep the collar and base of the plant free from damp as water drains straight through. At the same time it helps retain moisture beneath the surface.

Sweet Williams are generally treated as biennials and raised from seed in spring (see page 22), then planted out in their flowering positions in the autumn at 20–30cm (8–12in) apart. They will flower the following June. Thoroughly water them in their nursery rows the day before they are transplanted. Seeds can be started off in trays under glass in early spring and will then be ready for planting out in late spring after they have been hardened off. Annual carnations are also planted out in late spring from seeds sown under glass in mid- or late winter. These will flower through the summer from June onwards.

Aftercare Keep the beds as free from weeds as possible. These not only look unsightly and detract from the plants, but rob the soil of moisture and food. They also restrict the movement of air round the plants and provide refuges for pests. The best way of keeping them down is by hoeing or handweeding. Hoeing has the advantage that it breaks up the surface crust, allowing water to drain away quickly and air to penetrate the soil. Do not hoe too deeply as carnations are relatively shallow rooted so you could damage them. An inch (2.5cm) is quite deep enough.

The best way of keeping down weeds is by regular hoeing wih a Dutch hoe. Take care not to damage the young plants as you work.

Staking Carnations need very little attention during their first year. A single flowering shoot will be formed and need support. Border carnations are never 'stopped' (i.e. the leading shoot pinched out) in the way perpetual carnations and modern pinks are. Side shoots will begin to appear late in the first season and they will extend sufficiently to produce quite a number of flowers in the second season.

In the first year stake with just a single cane, supporting the flowering stem with split flower rings. In the second and subsequent years there are many more flowering stems to support, so use a special galvanized wire hoop attached to a cane or rod. Take care when putting in the cane that no damage is done to the roots. Alternatively, twiggy pea sticks can be used, provided you cut them before their leaves begin to expand. Pea sticks increase the bulk of the plants, so more space should be left between them at planting time if you intend using this method.

Disbudding This worries a lot of gardeners at first but it soon becomes second nature. If the flowers are primarily for garden decoration, it is not necessary to do any disbudding, except possibly around the terminal bud. If you intend to grow for cutting or for exhibition, then all buds beneath the terminal bud should be removed to provide a longer stem to cut. For safety reasons do not remove all the buds at once. Remove the lowest buds first and finally remove the second from top bud only when you are sure that the terminal bud is developing as it should.

There is no reason to disbud pinks, but it is a good idea to dead-head them as the remains of the flowers can make the plants look very shabby. With modern pinks, it also helps

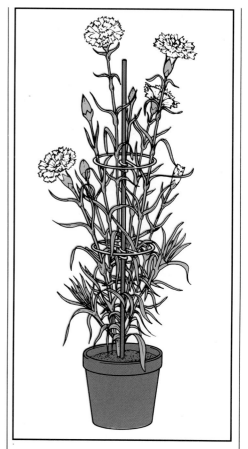

Galvanized wire hoops fixed to bamboo canes make excellent supports but do avoid root damage when inserting them.

prolong the flowering season. The same is true of species, except that you may wish to leave a few stems so you can collect some of the seed for future sowings.

Watering Carnations are not particularly thirsty plants, but you should water them in prolonged dry spells. Do not mulch with peat, leaves or straw as these tend to harbour pests and are also likely to cause rotting. Mulching species and pinks on rock gardens with gravel can be beneficial as mentioned earlier.

Feeding Similarly carnations and pinks are not gross feeders. Well rotted farmyard manure, garden compost or 'Forest Bark' Ground and Composted should be dug in when the bed is prepared and fertilizers can be applied in the growing season.

Some gardeners prefer to use a balanced general fertilizer such as ICI Liquid Growmore, others one that is high in potash. You can also buy specially formulated fertilizers produced particularly for use on carnations. Trial and error will help you make up your own mind, but whichever you decide to use, give it in the spring at the rate recommended on the packet. Then give a further application in the middle of the growing season.

Disbudding carnations gives better blooms for cutting and for show. All buds beneath the terminal bud are removed (near right). When side shoots develop, again remove all but the terminal bud (far right). A shoot before disbudding (below) and after the operation (below, far right).

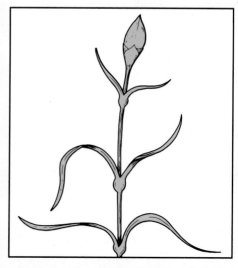

GROWING UNDER GLASS

Perpetual-flowering carnations and American spray carnations are usually grown under glass, though it is possible to stand them out in the open air during the summer.

The two basic requirements of light and air are as important inside greenhouses as they are out on the border, so bear this in mind. It's no good trying to grow carnations unless your greenhouse has adequate ventilation from low level side vents as well as roof vents. Glazing should extend to ground level to admit maximum light to the bases of the plants.

Heating Some form of heating will be required to keep the blooms in flower throughout the winter. Electric heaters are probably the easiest to use and if fitted with thermostats are reasonably cheap to run as they only come on when the temperature falls below the minimum required – 1°C (34°F) for survival, or 7°C (45°F) for constant flowering. They have the added advantage of having fans incorporated in them which keep the air circulating while all the vents are closed. Paraffin heaters are the alternative, but they are less controllable and can cause a very damp atmosphere. Heating costs can be kept to a minimum by providing the greenhouse with some form of double insulation, the cheapest being a polythene lining.

The greenhouse should be sited where it is not overhung by trees or in the shadow of tall walls.

While heat is to be kept in during the winter, excessive heat must be kept out during the summer. Adequate ventilation is essential and can be assisted in hot periods by the use of an electric fan. Light shading is also essential to keep out the hot sun. Blinds are the best as they can be adjusted, but they are expensive, so whitening the glass with a shading paint is usually sufficient.

The best type of greenhouse for carnations is one with glass which extends to ground level. This admits maximum light to the bases of the plants. It must also have good ventilation, from both side and roof vents.

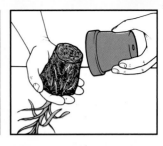

Young plants are started off in 8cm (3½in) pots. Later they should be transferred to 15cm (6in) pots. Use good compost. Root growth can be checked by carefully removing the pot.

Beds and pots Carnations can be grown in pots or specially prepared beds. The staging should be at a low level, not the conventional height, as they can grow up to 1.5m (5ft). If they are grown in beds it is sensible to provide access for a wheelbarrow to facilitate changing the soil.

Construct the beds on top of the soil level. Form them of wood, or aluminium strips which are longer lasting. The walls should be 15–20cm (6–8in) high. Line the beds with black polythene or, if a more permanent structure is envisaged, the base can be constructed from concrete or corrugated plastic sheeting. Whichever is used, make certain that it is even and slopes in one direction so that excess water readily drains away. As the beds are shallow it is not possible to use canes as supports. Erect cross bars at the end of each bed and stretch galvanized wires at 20cm (8in) intervals between them. Then tie strings across the wires, also 20cm (8in) apart, to form a grid through which the carnations grow.

Perpetuals can be grown to a good standard in pots. Clay pots were traditionally used, but they are now difficult to come by and also expensive. The advantage of clay pots is that they are less easily overwatered than plastic ones and they tend to keep the roots cooler in summer. Plastic pots retain water more readily so they can be overwatered. However, they do not dry out as quickly in hot weather and are also much easier to clean. Choice is a matter of preference.

Compost Carnations will grow equally well in soilless or loam-based composts. The choice is again a matter of personal preference and availability. If you have large beds to fill, you will perhaps want to use ordinary garden soil. This is quite acceptable so long as it is not too heavy. Mix well-rotted farmyard manure, garden compost or 'Forest Bark' Ground and Composted into the soil and add some crushed brick rubble or sharp sand to ensure good drainage. If the soil is on the acid side, add some lime or ground chalk to bring the pH level to within the range 6.5 to 7.

Planting and potting Plants can be obtained from specialist nurseries as rooted cuttings between mid-autumn and mid-spring or as 'stopped and broken' plants. These are established plants which have been stopped once and new shoots have broken from the base. Beginners will probably find it easier to start with these, as handling rooted cuttings needs a bit more experience.

Whether you have purchased rooted cuttings or produced your own, they should be potted into 8cm (3½in) pots and grown on until they have eight to ten fully developed pairs of leaves on the leading stem. Break this off cleanly at the sixth leaf joint, i.e. 'stop' it. Once this has been done, or you have received a purchased plant that has already been stopped, carefully pot it into a 15cm (6in) or 18cm (7in) pot, using good quality compost. Each pot should be 'crocked' – put pieces of broken pot or a layer of gravel in the bottom to assist free drainage. Water plants an hour before potting on and again afterwards. Then stand them on the low staging in the greenhouse.

If you plan to use beds, plant the 'stopped and broken' plants straight into them. Again water the plants before transplanting. Plant them out firmly at 20cm (8in) intervals with the top of the root ball level with the surface of the bed, then water in.

When young plants have eight to ten pairs of leaves on the main stem they should be stopped (right). This involves breaking off the tip of the stem at the sixth leaf (below). This stopping will result in the development of side shoots (below right).

Stopping and disbudding As soon as the newly emerged side shoots make eight to ten pairs of leaves it is time to consider the next step. There are three possible moves. All the shoots can be stopped again at the sixth pair of leaves so that each produces another set of side shoots, each of which will flower. It is preferable to stop the shoots at different times so they produce a succession of blooms, rather than make them all bloom at once by removing the tips simultaneously. The second method is to leave all the side shoots in to develop just one flower apiece. The third is a compromise between the two in which the lower half of the side shoots are removed. This is known as half-stopping.

As the plants are likely to grow 1.5m (5ft) tall they will need some support. Three or four canes can be inserted round the edges of the pots and string wound round them. The flowering stems then rise through this framework. It pays to attach the tops of the canes to a wire stretched along the greenhouse to prevent the top-heavy pots being knocked over. Wire supports for plants in beds have already been mentioned.

Disbudding perpetual-flowering carnations is done in the same way as for border carnations (see page 16). If American spray carnations are grown, the reverse procedure should be adopted: pinch out the terminal bud and let the rest develop into a full spray of blooms.

Aftercare Feeding and watering are essentially the same as for border carnations. Special carnation fertilizer can be obtained. Follow the directions on the packet but on no account overfeed the plants. Also avoid overwatering particularly if you are using plastic pots. Experience will soon teach you when to

When they are grown under glass, perpetual flowering carnations need plenty of light and air if quality blooms such as this are to be achieved.

water. It will be more frequent during hot weather than in wet muggy conditions. Water carefully in winter; little growth is taking place so less water is taken up. It is therefore better to err on the dry side rather than give the plants too much moisture round the roots.

Perpetual-flowering carnations will survive a winter at temperatures as low as 1°C (34°F), but they will not flower. For constant flowering throughout the cold months the temperature must be kept at a minimum of 7°C (45°F). This will require some heating as discussed earlier. In summer do not let the temperature rise much above 20°C (68°F) if it can be avoided. Good ventilation and shading will help with this.

PROPAGATION

Carnations and pinks must be among the easiest of all flowering plants to propagate. No special equipment is needed, though a heated propagating frame is an advantage. The three main methods for the amateur are from seed, by layering and from cuttings or pipings.

Seed All carnations and pinks can be grown from seed sown in January or February, but normally only annual carnations and species are propagated in this way. Vegetative means (such as cuttings or layering) are used to increase other forms of carnations and pinks as named varieties rarely come true from seed.

Fill seed trays with a compost such as 'Kericompost' and lightly tamp down. Spread the seeds thinly over the surface and then cover with a layer of sifted compost just sufficient to cover them. Then water the tray from below by standing it in water, but be careful that the water does not come over the rim of the tray. Seeds will germinate without heat but do so more quickly if a modicum of heat is given. This can be achieved by standing the trays in a heated propagator if you have one or keeping them in a heated greenhouse. Cover the trays with a piece of glass and a sheet of paper which should be removed as soon as the seeds start to germinate. Turn the glass each day to clear condensed moisture. When the seedlings appear give them ample light but keep them away from strong sunlight.

Seedlings should be pricked out into trays of potting compost 5cm (2in) apart or into 7.5cm (3in) pots. Harden them off before planting them out.

Sweet Williams (*Dianthus barbatus*) can be sown outdoors in nursery rows. Prepare a seedbed with a good tilth, which means that the surface soil should be broken down finely, and sow the seeds thinly in shallow drills. When the seedlings appear they should be thinned out to 15cm (6in) apart. Sweet Williams are sown outside in mid- to late spring for planting out the following autumn or

PROPAGATION OF CARNATIONS AND PINKS

	Border Carnation	Perpetual-flowering Carnation	American Spray Carnation	Annual Carnations
SEEDS	X	X		XX
LAYERS	XX			
CUTTINGS	X	XX	XX	X

they can be sown under glass in early spring for planting out in late spring.

Annual carnations are normally sown in mid- or late winter for transplanting in late spring, but they can also be sown in the autumn for earlier flowering if you wish.

Layering Border carnations can be grown from seed, but it is essential to use vegetative means to perpetuate named varieties. Though it is possible to strike cuttings, a greater success rate comes from layering after flowering is over.

Annual dianthus, such as this attractive fimbriated variety, are normally sown in mid- or late winter for transplanting in late spring.

Old-fashioned Pinks	Modern Pinks	Species	
		XX	
X	X		**XX Preferred method**
XX	XX	XX	**X Also possible**

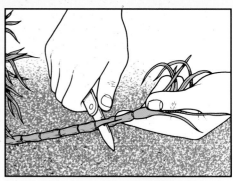

1 Border carnations can be propagated by layering after flowering.

2 Remove lower leaves from a strong shoot, then cut a tongue.

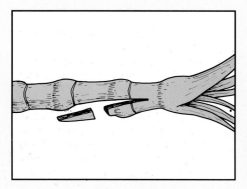

3 When the stem is bent this tongue will open out. Roots will form from cut tissue.

4 Make a hole near parent plant and fill with sandy compost.

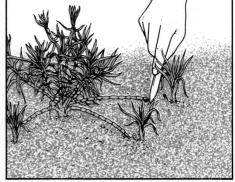

5 Secure the stem in the hole with a wire layering pin and cover with soil.

6 After five or six weeks the rooted layer can be removed and planted elsewhere.

Make a shallow trench or a series of holes round the parent plant and fill these with compost made of equal parts loam, peat and sharp sand. This mixture should be firmed in and watered. Select a strong shoot and carefully remove its lower leaves, leaving the top six pairs. Insert a pointed knife into the stem just below the bottom remaining leaves and draw it downwards and out of the stem immediately below the next joint or node. When bent this will produce a tongue of stem. This should be neatly trimmed back to the base of node.

The stem should be gently bent downwards and inserted into the compost, so that the open tongue and part of the stem are covered. Hold it in position with a layering pin – just a bent piece of wire shaped like a hairpin. Press the compost firmly over the layered portion. Each plant will supply several shoots suitable for layering and these should be dealt with in turn around the plant. The layers should be watered in and then prevented from drying out too much at any time.

Allow five or six weeks for the layers to root, then they can be severed from the parent plant. After about another week they can be lifted and potted up.

It is possible to layer plants that are kept in pots. Follow the same procedure but peg down the stem into the edge of the pot after replacing some of its compost with the mixture used for layering out of doors.

Cuttings An alternative vegetative method of producing plants that are true replicas of their parents is by striking cuttings. All carnations and pinks can be propagated in this way, but it is more usual for perpetual-flowering carnations and pinks.

The same basic technique can be used for all types, but the timing of the operation varies. The best time for taking cuttings of perpetual-flowering carnations is from early to late winter but for pinks this should be early to late summer. Border carnations can also be struck during the summer period.

Cuttings taken in winter will need a heated propagator to encourage them to root. You can buy one ready made or you could build your own using soil-heating cables in a home-made propagator. No heat is required in summer and cuttings can then be struck in pots or even in the open ground. Cutting compost is a straightforward mix of equal parts peat and sharp sand.

Cuttings should be prepared promptly and not left to wilt. If they are being collected in the open garden put them into a polythene bag until they are used. The best cuttings are obtained from young plants, which should be vigorous and disease free. For perpetuals choose side shoots from the middle part of the main stem. Snap each shoot off cleanly from the second node, leaving two pairs of leaves on the plant from which new shoots will emerge. An older method is to remove the side shoot completely taking with it a slight heel from the main stem. Trim this heel with a sharp knife and remove the lowest pair of leaves.

Dip the base of each cutting in a hormone rooting powder such as 'Keriroot', then insert them round the edge of a pot or in a tray and put them in a propagator. Keep the sand in the base of the propagator at a constant 13°C (55°F) and keep the atmosphere humid by spraying the cuttings once or twice a day. In the second week increase the ventilation and cease spraying. After four weeks the plants should be rooted and ready for potting up.

The heat can be dispensed with in

1 Carnations and pinks can be increased from cuttings of side shoots.

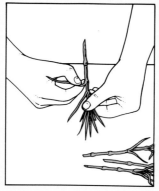

2 Remove the lowest leaves from the cutting by pulling them off.

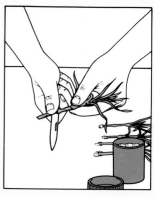

3 Any heel on a cutting should be trimmed cleanly with a sharp knife.

4 The prepared cuttings are inserted around the edge of a pot with the aid of a dibber, and using cutting compost.

summer. Stand the pots in a sunless but well-lit position and spray the plants occasionally with water during the first fortnight. After four to six weeks the rooted cuttings should be ready for potting up. If the cuttings are not taken until the autumn and you give them no heat delay potting up until the spring.

Cuttings of pinks can be taken in exactly the same way, or they can be made by simply pulling the stem apart at a node, like pulling a plug from a socket, instead of snapping it. Cuttings of this kind are referred to as pipings.

Division Border plants can be divided by first piling soil in the centre of each plant, then splitting them when new roots have been formed on the now underground stems. This is only a crude form of layering and has little to recommend it.

January/February Little need be done outside except to check that frost has not lifted young plants out of the ground and that the wind has not piled damp leaves round the plants. Inside temperatures should be kept above 7°C (45°F), with adequate ventilation on warm days. Take cuttings from perpetual-flowering carnations. Sow annual carnations. Continue enjoying flowers cut regularly from the greenhouse.

March/April Top-dress the borders with a general fertilizer, and lightly hoe. Rock garden pinks can be top-dressed with a little fertilizer and a gravel mulch. If planting out was delayed in autumn it can now be undertaken. Prepare beds for autumn planting. Sow border carnations in open beds. Sow Sweet Williams under glass to plant out in late spring. Pot up any rooted cuttings and stop young plants. Watch the temperature in the greenhouse – it may rise too high on sunny days.

May Regular hoeing and hand-weeding in the borders. Plant out annual carnations and Sweet Williams grown under glass. Sow Sweet Williams in open beds. Stake border carnations. Pot on the perpetual-flowering carnations. Start regular feeding of second-year plants.

Rock garden pinks can be topdressed with a little fertilizer and a gravel mulch during March or April.

June/July Border carnations and pinks in flower. Deadhead to promote flowering. Take pipings of pinks and layer border carnations. Water if necessary. Keep weeds under control. Shade greenhouse and in hot weather syringe perpetual carnations, but keep water off the flowers. Provide maximum ventilation. Check plants under glass regularly for watering, feeding, disbudding and supporting. Keep a look-out for pests and deal with them quickly.

August Tidy up pink and border carnation plants after they have finished flowering. Continue to deadhead modern pinks. There is still time to take pipings from pinks and layer border carnations (see page 24). Remove Sweet Williams that have finished flowering. Pot on perpetual-flowering carnations if necessary. Continue to keep the greenhouse atmosphere moist and appropriately ventilated during any spells of hot weather.

Border pinks, such as this Allwoodii variety 'Diane', should be deadheaded regularly as this encourages more flowers.

The main flowering period of border carnations is early and mid-summer. For garden display they should not be disbudded.

Hardy dianthus of all kinds are excellent for cottage-style gardens, looking particularly charming if they spill on to old brick paths or York paving.

September/October Sever rooted layers of border carnations and pot up. Finalize new beds for these and pinks and plant out. Transplant Sweet Williams from their nursery beds to flowering positions. Give borders final hoeing and hand weeding. Tidy up the plants by cutting them back and removing any dead growth or leaves. Purchase new perpetual carnations for inside and discard any three-year-old plants. Watch for falling night-time temperatures.

November/December Finish the tidying up of beds if the weather permits. Remove any damp, fallen leaves that have blown round the plants. Pot up any late layered carnations and protect under glass for the winter. Prepare beds for spring planting. Keep greenhouse temperatures above 7°C (45°F) if continued flowering is required. Remove greenhouse shading. Start taking cuttings of perpetual-flowering carnations. Control watering as growth slows.

PESTS AND DISEASES

Two essentials in the fight against pests and diseases are the selection of healthy stock and maintaining hygienic conditions around the plants, with plenty of air and light. If these elementary precautions are taken the following list will not be as daunting as it might first appear.

PESTS

Aphids (greenfly and blackfly) These insects suck the plants' sap. They are easily controlled with an insecticide based on pirimicarb such as 'Rapid' which does not harm beneficial insects.

Carnation fly This attacks plants under glass and in the open. The maggots of this fly burrow into the leaves which should be removed without delay and burnt.

Red spider mite These minute insects attack the leaves, which soon turn brown and die, and eventually kill the whole plant. They attack mainly during dry, hot weather. You can reduce the risk of attack by keeping the atmosphere moist during hot weather. Control is difficult, but fumigate the greenhouse with a 'Fumite' General Purpose Insecticide Smoke or spraying with 'Sybol' helps.

Thrips Attacks outdoor and indoor plants, damaging the blooms, within which the eggs are laid. Spray with malathion or 'Sybol'.

Tortrix moth This moth's caterpillar feeds on all parts of the plant causing great damage, particularly to the buds. At first sighting, spray with 'Picket' or 'Sybol'.

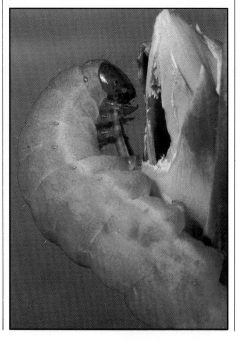

ABOVE Fine pale speckling on carnation foliage caused by red spider mite. These pests attack mainly during dry, hot weather.

RIGHT Caterpillars can attack flower buds of carnations, and indeed all parts of the plants. They cause great damage if not controlled.

FUNGAL DISEASES

A number of fungal diseases attack carnations, most of them prevalent in damp, airless conditions. Remove affected parts of the plants and spray the whole plant with a fungicide such as Benlate + 'Activex'. Check that the ventilation is adequate. The commonest fungal diseases are listed below.

Anther smut The anthers, in the centre of the flower, turn black.

Fairy ring spot Yellowish spots on the leaves, with dark rings of spores radiating from their centres.

Leaf rot Leaves rot near the base.

Leaf spot Brownish, circular spots with a darker, purplish edging.

Mildew A white, powdery fungus, usually found in late summer.

Rust A very common fungal disease in carnations. Dark brown spores appear on the leaves, then on other parts of the plant.

Stem rots and wilts A variety of fungal and bacterial diseases which cause yellowing, wilting and rotting of the plant. The whole plant should be destroyed and the soil replaced or sterilized as the diseases are infectious. Never take cuttings from such plants. Rot can also result from bad drainage. It is not then infectious and can be simply remedied.

OTHER PROBLEMS

Virus diseases The leaves have a yellow, mottled or streaked appearance and the affected plants lose vigour. Burn the plants. The diseases are usually transmitted by greenfly and other pests, so keep these under control. Never take cuttings from infected stock.

Split calyx Petals pour out through splits in the calyx giving a lop-sided appearance. This can be caused by a variety of things, including fluctuating temperatures, incorrect feeding and excessive watering. Calyx rings or bands can be bought from specialist nurseries and slipped over the growing buds to prevent this.

SIXTY OF THE BEST

From the vast range of varieties that you can buy here are 60 of the best carnations and pinks available from specialist nurseries and good garden centres throughout the country.

The British National Carnation Society
3 Canberra Close,
Hornchurch, Essex

The Society issues an annual yearbook and keeps members informed on all aspects of the cultivation of carnations and pinks.

Spring, summer and autumn shows are held at the Royal Horticultural Society's Hall at Westminster.

BORDER CARNATIONS
Selfs
'**Aldridge Yellow**' Bright canary yellow. A strong grower with large flowers. Awarded the Award of Merit (A.M.) in 1951. Other good yellows to look for include 'Beauty of Cambridge', 'Brimstone', 'Mary Murray' and 'Sunray'.

'**Belle of Bookham**' A very attractive shade of old rose with a silvery sheen. Strong grower and good for exhibitions.

'**Bookham Perfume**' Crimson red. Like so many of the 'Bookham' strains, this is an old favourite, one of its attractions being its strong scent. There are several other perfumed crimsons of note, including 'Black Douglas Clove', 'Downs Crimson', 'Fingo Clove', 'Gypsy Clove' and 'Old Crimson Clove'.

'**Consul**' A rich flame apricot, almost orange. A very fine plant for the open border in all weathers with its compact habit. Awarded the A.M. in 1951. Other apricots worth considering include 'Bookham Apricot', 'Clunie', 'Flameau', 'Lustre'.

'**Edenside White**' Pure white. Very popular for its compact habit, large flowers and fine scent. It was awarded an A.M. in 1951. Although the colour most often associated with carnations, there are not many good whites available. Others well worth trying include 'Eudoxia', 'Snow Clove', 'Spindrift' and 'Whitecliff'.

'**Fiery Cross**' A really good brilliant scarlet. A strong, vigorous grower which won a well-deserved A.M. in 1955. Good for showing at exhibitions. Several other very fine scarlets that are worth growing

34

include 'Fusilie', 'Oscar', 'Scarlet Fragrance', 'Tally Ho' and 'W.B. Cranfield'.

'Frances Sellars' A rose pink. Another old favourite and a strong grower with a good habit. It was awarded an A.M. in 1947. Other good pink selfs worth considering are 'Bookham Peach', 'Cherry Clove', 'Clarinda', 'Ibis', 'Mayhole' and 'Pink Clove'.

'Lord Grey' Variously described as heliotrope-grey or mauve. This

The vigorous 'Fiery Cross'.

Border fancy 'Peter Wood'.

grey-mauve is the nearest that border carnations come to being blue. Other good varieties to look for include 'Antiquary', 'Clarabelle' and 'Lavender Clove'.

Picotees
'Eva Humphries' A perfect pure white flower with a delicate wire edge of purple. This is an extremely attractive plant that has retained its popularity. Awarded the F.C.C. in 1947. One of its parents was another old favourite, 'Fair Maiden', again a white ground, but this time with a scarlet edge. Another good white with a purple edge that has much to recommend it is 'Fascination'.

'Firefly' This is a cultivar with a good yellow ground, heavily edged with crimson-claret. It was awarded an F.C.C. in 1941. Another excellent yellow, but with a less prominent purple edge is 'Santa Claus'.

Fancies
'A.A. Sanders' A very good old variety with an orange ground, broadly edged and marked with heliotrope grey and splashed with red. It was awarded an A.M. in 1947. Other good orange-ground varieties include 'Douglas Fancy' (edged blood-red), 'Fancy Monarch' (pale purple markings), 'Horsa' (scarlet markings), 'Orange Maid' (flaked with bronze) and 'Peter Wood'.

Plant Awards
Plants of particular merit have been given awards by the Royal Horticultural Society. The following are mentioned in this list:-

A.M.   Award of Merit
F.C.C.   First Class Certificate

'Bookham Heroine' A superb plant with a clear shrimp-pink ground suffused with bright cherry red. Another very good pink is 'Mendip Hills' (flaked brilliant scarlet).

'Harmony' A heliotrope-lavender grey with cerise stripes. This unusual colour mixture is an old favourite and still well worth growing. Awarded an F.C.C. in 1937.

'Robin Thain' This is one of the best white ground fancies which is flaked rosy-crimson and has a very strong scent. It is vigorous but has a neat habit. Its F.C.C. was awarded in 1946. Other fine white grounds well worth considering include 'Alice Forbes Improved' (with rosy-mauve stripes), 'Bookham Lad' (scarlet stripes), 'Candy Clove' (rosy-red stripes, strongly scented), 'Dainty Lady' (pencilled red stripes), 'Mary Simpster' (rose markings), 'Merlin Clove' (purple stripes, and strongly scented).

'Zebra' This is a very attractive variety with a maize-yellow ground striped with crimson-maroon. A very old favourite of good shape and habit. Other yellow ground fancies well worth looking out for include 'Bookham Fancy' edged and ticked carmine-purple, 'Catherine Glover' edged and barred with scarlet, 'Happiness', edged with scarlet, 'Sunstar' which is both edged and striped with bright scarlet.

PERPETUAL-FLOWERING CARNATIONS
Crimson
'Joker' This is probably the best of the crimson varieties and certainly a great favourite. The large blooms are a rich dark colour with deeply serrated petals and produced on strong, wiry stems. The growth is vigorous and free-flowering. It is a short variety.

'Allwoods Crimson' An exhibition variety with very large blooms. It has the benefit of a strong scent. It is of medium stature.

Other worthy crimson varieties to look out for include 'Alec Sparkes', 'Bailey's Masterpiece', 'Crimson Velvet' and 'Topsy'.

'Joker', perpetual variety.

Perpetual 'Dusty Sim'.

Perpetual 'Lavender Lady'.

Lavender, mauve and purple
'Persian Pink' 'Pink' is a bit misleading here as this is lavender-pink tending towards mauve. A very free-flowering variety of strong growth. Tall.

'Lavender Lady' Pale lavender of fine colour. Rather short in stature.

Other varieties to choose from include 'Deep Purple', 'La Royale', 'Orchid Mauve', 'Purple Frosted' and 'Storm'.

Pink
'Bailey's Splendour' A pearly shade of pink with well-formed blooms, suitable for decorative or exhibition purposes. It has a very good short, compact habit.

'Dusty Sim' A most unusual shade of dusty pastel pink that is extremely useful for decorative purposes. It is of medium growth with large flowers.

There are many fine pinks to

Perpetual 'J.M. Bibby'.

choose from. These include 'Crowley Sim', 'Fragrant Rose' (scented), 'Laddie Sim', 'Lena', 'Linda', 'Pink Sim', 'Shocking Pink'.

Scarlet
'J.M. Bibby' An outstanding carnation for exhibiting with large, well shaped blooms and compact habit. Medium height.

Perpetual-flowering 'William Sim'.

'Robert Allwood' The blooms are large and of a brilliant scarlet colour. It makes short, bushy growth.

'Scania' Another very fine bright scarlet which does not fade, making it a good cut flower. Tall in growth.

'William Sim' One of the all-time favourites. Very bright scarlet of top quality and strong growth. It was originally introduced under the name 'Farida'.

Scarlet is a popular colour and there are many other good varieties including 'Astor' and 'Cardinal Sim'.

White
'Fragrant Anne' Pure white with outstanding perfume, possibly the best. A large-flowered variety suitable for exhibiting. Compact habit and of short stature.

Well-scented 'Fragrant Anne'.

'White Sim' The most popular of the whites as it is both vigorous and prolific flowering. Tall in growth.

Other whites of top quality include 'George Allwood', 'Ice Cap' and 'Northland'.

Perpetual-flowering 'Tangerine Sim'.

Yellow
'Golden Rain' A very good yellow. Free-flowering with bushy growth and strong stems. Short.

'Harvest Moon' A rich golden yellow. A free-flowering variety and of medium height.

The yellows vary from apricot to orange. Other varieties in this range include 'Mandarin Sim', 'Tangerine Sim' and 'Yellow Dusty'.

Fancies
'Arthur Sim' This has a white ground with red stripes. It yields a profusion of large blooms so it makes an excellent cut flower. Tall. Other white grounds worth considering include 'Danna Brogg' (edged and flecked in scarlet), 'New Arthur' (red stripes), 'Red Diamond' (red stripes).

The perpetual 'Arthur Sim'.

The 'Knight' series of annual carnation includes white blooms.

The annual 'Knight' series.

'**Cocomo Sim**' A yellow-apricot ground with scarlet stripes. Very free-flowering. Tall. Other yellow-ground fancies include 'Marina' (paler coloured bands), 'Pallas' (deep pink flecks), 'Skyline' (red flakes), 'Spotlight' (flecked with pink), 'Telstar' (bright red stripes).

'**Doris Allwood**' A wonderful combination of colours with rose-pink stripes and bars on a French-grey ground. With a fine strong clove scent as well, this is an excellent plant. It makes compact growth and is short in stature.

'**Flame Sim**' Yet another 'Sim', this time with a scarlet ground and scarlet flakes. Tall. Other good red grounds to consider are 'Anne Marie' (white edging and lines) and 'G.J. Sim' (dark pink with white lines).

AMERICAN SPRAY CARNATIONS
'**Exquisite**' Dark purple with a paler edge. A good strong scent makes it a popular cut flower.

'**Heidi**' White with a delicate red picotee edging and markings.

'**Scarlet Elegance**' Bright scarlet fading to white at the petal edges.

'**White Elegance**' Pure white with a good scent.

ANNUAL CARNATIONS

'Chabaud' or 'Marguerite' carnations were first developed in 1870 and are still the best known. Giant Chabauds are commonly bought as mixed seed, but it is still occasionally possible to obtain individual colours. Their one big drawback is that they tend to burst their calyces. There are Dwarf Chabauds, again sold in mixed colours, which are more compact, growing to 40cm (16in).

Two slightly newer strains are 'Giant of Nice' and 'Enfant de Nice'. These are taller, stronger smelling and with better colours; they make good carnations for cutting.

A very fine recent introduction has been the 'Knight' series which produces dwarf compact plants. A variety of colours is available and most are strongly perfumed. They make very good cut flowers.

OLD-FASHIONED PINKS

'Bridal Veil' A pink from the seventeenth century which has pure white double flowers with a light crimson patch at the base of each fringed petal. It is heavily scented.

'Charles Musgrave' Another good seventeenth-century plant that has been known by many names, including 'Avalon', 'Washfield', 'Musgrave's Pink' and 'Green Eye'. The last is particularly apt as it does have a conspicuous green zone or eye at the centre of each pure white, single flower. The petals are fringed and it has a magnificent perfume.

'Earl of Essex' A very popular Victorian pink. It is double with fringed petals of fine rose-pink. It has a tendency to split its calyx, as do so many old-fashioned pinks, but its colour, beautiful scent and free-flowering more than compensate.

'Emile Pare' A mid-nineteenth century plant from France. It bears clusters of double, clear salmon-pink flowers. Not long lived, so it needs regular propagation, preferably every year, to insure against its loss.

Old-fashioned pink 'Charles Musgrave': highly scented.

'Fimbriata' Possibly dating from Elizabethan times. Its double flowers are creamy white with fringed petals and a strong perfume. It tends to be a bit untidy, as the double flower is so full it often bursts its calyx in its exuberance.

'Inchmery' A magnificent plant dating from the eighteenth century. It is a beautiful silvery, shell pink, set off by compact, silvery foliage. It is semi-double with plain petals that open wide. The final ingredient is a wonderful and memorable fragrance.

Dianthus **'Mrs Sinkins'.**

'Montrose Pink' This pink came from Montrose House in Fife and was first recorded there in the early eighteenth century. It is a neat plant with double red flowers complemented by a darker red centre. It is also known as 'Cockensie'.

'Mrs Sinkins' One of the all-time favourites. Raised in Victorian times, this is a pure white double blessed with the most beautiful scent. It is a bit untidy in habit and the calyces tend to burst under the abundance of petals, but it is the quintessence of a cottage garden. There is a pink version raised in more recent times.

'Pheasant Eye' Another pink from Elizabethan times. This is known both in single and semi-double forms, each having deeply serrated petals with a white or slight pinkish ground and a deep purple-brown centre or eye. The markings are variable and it occasionally has a laced edge too.

Dianthus **'Inchmery', a magnificent 18th century plant.**

'Sam Barlow' A favourite Victorian pink. It has a large double white flower with a maroon blotch at its centre which is so dark as to appear almost black. It is particularly noted for its fine scent.

'Sops-in-Wine' One of the oldest pinks still in existence, dating from the fourteenth century. There seem to be many contenders for this name, but my favourite 'Sop-in-Wine' is a very heavily serrated double white with the same almost black centre as 'Sam Barlow'. It has a very strong clove scent.

Other versions of this pink include lacing of the same black-red. In medieval times it was used to flavour wine.

'White Ladies' A most prolific flowering pink from the last century with very deeply fringed double white flowers. Unlike most of the old-fashioned pinks it has quite a lengthy flowering season and – another point in its favour – it does not split its calyces so readily. Ideal as an edging plant and can be left undisturbed for years.

MODERN AND SHOW PINKS

'Doris' The best of the Allwoodii modern pinks with its semi-double salmon-pink flower with a reddish eye at the centre. Its fragrant blooms have a very long season, right into the winter in some years, making it a very welcome cut flower. Recently new sports from 'Doris' have given rise to 'Doris Elite', 'Doris Majestic' and 'Doris Supreme' which could very well provide a challenge to her popularity.

'Freckles' Has a dusky salmon-pink ground covered with red flecks. A very compact attractive plant.

Allwoodii pink 'Doris'.

The modern pink 'Freckles'.

Modern pink 'Haytor' has outstanding fragrance.

'Haytor White' A pure white double flower with serrated petals. The blooms are fairly large compared with most pinks and this, plus its fine fragrance, makes it a good cut flower. It has a long season.

'Joy' Deep salmon pink with deeply fringed petals and a fine scent. Very free-flowering and an excellent cut flower.

'Letitia Wyatt' Pale pink double flowers with a very strong scent. A new, but popular, variety.

'London Delight' Mauve with a purple eye and clove scented. One of a whole range of delightful pinks prefaced with 'London'. Other good examples are 'London Girl' (white with almost black lacing and eye), 'London Lovely' (white with mauve lacing and a darker eye) and 'London Poppet' (white/pink with ruby-red lacing and eye).

The pink 'London Delight'.

'Show Ideal' Creamy white with a pink flush and salmon-pink eye. Originally bred for showing purposes this is really intermediate between pinks and carnations. Other members of this group include 'Show Aristocrat' (flesh pink, buff eye), 'Show Beauty' (deep rose pink, maroon eye), 'Show Exquisite' (carmine rose, and darker centre), 'Show Pearl', (pure white), 'Show Portrait' (deep cardinal red, scented).

SPECIES

Dianthus alpinus A very varied species giving rise to many good garden hybrids. The colours vary from white to dark red or purple, sometimes with eyes or other markings. They form neat clumps about 10cm (4in) high and flower during midsummer. Raise from seed, but propagate good forms from cuttings. Hybrids worth growing include 'Bombardier' (very dark crimson, semi-double), 'Dainty Maid' (red, crimson eye), 'Elizabeth' (rose-pink, dark eye), 'Mars' (red double) and 'Pike's Pink' (pale pink double).

Dianthus barbatus The well-known Sweet William. A perennial which is normally treated as a biennial and used as a bedding plant. It flowers in early summer after being raised from seed in mid- to late spring of the previous year. Colours vary from white to a red that is almost black. Fortunately there are many named varieties which come true from seed. Hybrids are also available, the best known of which is 'Sweet Wivelsfield' which has larger flowers than the true species.

Dianthus gratianopolitanus Our rare native Cheddar Pink. Deep rose-pink with deeply fringed petals and a wonderful scent. Longer lived than most other species, but can be propagated from seed or cuttings. Previously known as *D. caesius*, under which name it can still be found.

Dianthus gratianopolitanus

Dianthus barbatus **hybrid 'Sweet Wivelsfield'.**

'Snowfire', a variety of the Indian pink.

Indian pink 'Baby Doll'.

Dianthus chinensis (Japanese or Indian Pink). This is commonly seen in the range of 'Heddewigii' cultivars which show great diversity in colour and form. The single or double flowers cover the complete colour range from white to crimson, and can be single or multicoloured. They are normally treated as annuals for bedding out but can be kept for a second year. A large range can be seen in seed catalogues, but good strains are 'Baby Doll', 'Magic Charms', 'Queen of Hearts' and 'Snowfire'.

46

Dianthus deltoides (Maiden Pink) A pretty rock garden plant suitable for growing in paving with a good range of colours from white to red. It is normally grown from seed, but once established it will seed itself quite happily. Selected varieties are available which will come reasonably true from seed as long as they are not planted too close to each other. Good strains to search out are 'Albus', 'Bowles Variety', 'Brilliant', 'Flashing Lights' and 'Wisley Variety'.

Dianthus deltoides 'Brilliant'.

A good strain of *Dianthus deltoides*:'Flashing Lights'.

INDEX AND ACKNOWLEDGEMENTS

Picture credits

Pat Brindley: 6(t,b),8(t,b),9(t,b),14(b), 23,38(t),40(t,b),43(t).
Harry Smith Horticultural Photographic Collection: 1,10,11,13(t,b),
    14(t),29,32/3,39(b),42(t).
Michael Warren: 21,27,28(t,b),30(bl,br),31(tl,tr),34,35(t,b),36(l,r),
    37(t,b),39(t),41,42(b),43(b).
Colin Watmough: 38(b).

Artwork by Simon Roulstone